GIRL'S EDITION

KIDS' MUSICAL THEATRE AUDITION

INCLUDES A CD OF FULL PERFORMANCES & ACCOMPANIMENTS
COMPILED AND ARRANGED BY **MICHAEL DANSICKER**

ISBN-13: 978-1-4234-2877-0
ISBN-10: 1-4234-2877-3

7777 W. BLUEMOUND RD. P.O. BOX 13819 MILWAUKEE, WI 53213

The following song is the property of:

Bourne Co.
Music Publishers
5 West 37th Street
New York, NY 10018

I'VE GOT NO STRINGS

For all works contained herein:
Unauthorized copying, arranging, adapting, recording or public performance is an infringement of copyright.
Infringers are liable under the law.

Visit Hal Leonard Online at
www.halleonard.com

PREFACE

This collection of songs has been compiled and arranged specifically to provide interesting, performable material to be used in the audition situation. In addition to the musical challenges of each piece, there is a dramatic unity and specificity in each number that greatly complements the singing element. The accompaniments are supportive of the lyrical content but do not always double the vocal line. To deliver a polished audition, the young performer must spend rehearsal time with a vocal coach, pianist, or the included recorded accompaniments.

To comply with the time limitations of a professional audition, each number is to be performed as presented, without any internal repetition. The keys have been selected to show a full vocal range: Boys (unchanged voices) and Girls (belt and head voice.) And happily, teenagers (along with pre-teens) will find this material a very useful addition to their repertoire and a great deal of fun to perform.

While the music selected is from the world of traditional musical theatre, the adaptation and arrangements are presented with a contemporary sensibility. These arrangements have been carefully developed over an extended period of time and have been very successful in helping a number of young singing actors realize their performance goals. At the request of many casting directors and agents, I am making this material available to everyone for the first time.

Whether auditioning for the spring school musical or a professional Broadway show, you will be on the right track performing any of the included songs. And perhaps these editions will help provide an answer to that most frequently asked question: "What should I sing at my audition?"

Michael Dansicker
New York City
September, 2007

Michael Dansicker
Arranger, composer, music director, orchestrator, and pianist on more than 100 Broadway and Off-B'way productions: from ALL NIGHT STRUT ('77) to Bob Dylan's THE TIMES THEY ARE A-CHANGIN' ('06). In the world of concert dance he has worked with Jerome Robbins, Agnes DeMille, Twyla Tharp, Geoffrey Holder, ABT, and the Joffrey. FILM(vocal supervisor): ELF, MEET THE PARENTS, ANALYZE THAT and scored the dances for Paramount's BRAIN DONORS. He is currently arranging and scoring the international dance production: AMERICAN DANCE! ('08) directed by Kenny Ortega. In addition to the many vocal tracks he has produced for Hal Leonard Corporation, he has created THE AUDITION SUITE (with Martin Charnin) and THE 16-BAR THEATRE AUDITION (4 volumes).

TABLE OF CONTENTS

PAGE	TITLE	SHOW/FILM	CD Full Performance	CD Full Accompanniment
8	Baby Face		1	11
12	Button Up Your Overcoat	*Follow Thru*	2	12
5	I Always Knew	*Annie Warbucks*	3	13
16	I've Got No Strings	*Pinocchio*	4	14
18	My Buddy		5	15
21	Never Never Land	*Peter Pan*	6	16
24	Somebody Loves Me	*George White's Scandals 1924*	7	17
27	Who Do You Love I Hope	*Annie Get Your Gun*	8	18
30	Won't You Charleston with Me?	*The Boyfriend*	9	19
34	You're Never Fully Dressed Without a Smile	*Annie*	10	20

Singers on the CD:
Lila Coogan (tracks 5, 7, 9), **Brooke Greenberg** (2, 4, 6), **Lindsay Maron** (1, 3, 8, 10)

Piano:
Lawrence Yurman

Piano and Vocal Tracks recorded at: P.P.I. Recording, Inc., New York City
Tracks Engineered by Chip M. Fabrizi
Piano and Vocal Tracks produced by Michael Dansicker
Special thank you to: Amelia DeMayo

ON THE CD

Lila Coogan

Theatre Credits: AMERICAN GIRL & CIRCLE OF FRIENDS at The American Girl Theatre, LES MISÉRABLES (Westchester Broadway Theatre), 5,000 FINGERS OF DR. T.

Brooke Greenberg

Theatre Credits: ANNIE JR., XMAS CAROL, and HIGH SCHOOL MUSICAL at the Helen Hayes Theatre. Recording: TWO CITIES (soundtrack), HOW TO EAT LIKE A CHILD, UNCLE HENRY'S MUSIC.

Linsday Maron

Theatre Credit: AMERICAN GIRL THEATRE. Featured on recordings KIDZ BOP, CDs 9, 19 & Goldies, and also BARBIE POP.

Lawrence Yurman

Musical Director: GREY GARDENS. He has played and conducted the Broadway Productions of THOROUGHLY MODERN MILLIE, SIDE SHOW, and LES MISÉRABLES; and the Off-Broadway TWENTY FINGERS, TWENTY TOES! He is an active coach and accompanist in New York City.

I'VE GOT NO STRINGS
from Walt Disney's *Pinocchio*

Words by Ned Washington
Music by Leigh Harline

NEVER NEVER LAND
from *Peter Pan*

Lyric by Betty Comden and Adolph Green
Music by Jule Styne
Arranged by Michael Dansicker

© 1954 (Renewed) BETTY COMDEN, ADOLPH GREEN and JULE STYNE
All Rights Controlled by EDWIN H. MORRIS & COMPANY, A Division of MPL Music Publishing, Inc.
All Rights Reserved

SOMEBODY LOVES ME
from *George White's Scandals of 1924*

Words by B.G. DeSylva and Ballard MacDonald
Music by George Gershwin
Arranged by Michael Dansicker

Copyright © 1924 Stephen Ballentine Music and Warner Bros. Inc.
Copyright Renewed
All Rights for Stephen Ballentine Music Administered by The Songwriters Guild Of America
International Copyright Secured   All Rights Reserved

YOU'RE NEVER FULLY DRESSED WITHOUT A SMILE

from the Musical Production *Annie*

Lyrics by Martin Charnin
Music by Charles Strouse
Arranged by Michael Dansicker

© 1977 (Renewed) EDWIN H. MORRIS & COMPANY, A Division of MPL Music Publishing, Inc. and CHARLES STROUSE
Worldwide publishing on behalf of CHARLES STROUSE owned by CHARLES STROUSE PUBLISHING (Administered by WILLIAMSON MUSIC)
All Rights Reserved   Used by Permission
www.CharlesStrouse.com

HAL LEONARD HAS MANY BOOKS OF SOLOS FOR CHILDREN

Highlights include:

Girl's Songs from Musicals
HL00001126

Boy's Songs from Musicals
HL00001127

Children's Sacred Solos
HL00740297

Christmas Solos for Kids
HL00740130

Church Solos for Kids
HL00740080

Disney Solos for Kids
HL00740197

More Disney Solos for Kids
HL00740294

Kids' Broadway Songbook
HL00740149 Book/CD Pack
HL00331609 Book only
HL 00740316 Accomp. CD only

Popular Solos for Young Singers
HL00740150 Book/CD Pack
HL00740777 Book only
00740317 Accomp. CD only

ABOUT THE ENHANCED CD

In addition to piano accompaniments playable on both your CD player and computer, this enhanced CD also includes tempo adjustment and transposition software for computer use only. This software, known as Amazing Slow Downer, was originally created for use in pop music to allow singers and players the freedom to independently adjust both tempo and pitch elements. Because we believe there may be valuable educational use for these features in classical and theatre music, we have included this software as a tool for both the teacher and student. For quick and easy installation instructions of this software, please see below.

In recording a piano accompaniment we necessarily must choose one tempo. Our choice of tempo, phrasing, *ritardandos*, and dynamics is carefully considered. But by the nature of recording, it is only one option.

However, we encourage you to explore your own interpretive ideas, which may differ from our recordings. This new software feature allows you to adjust the tempo up and down without affecting the pitch. Likewise, Amazing Slow Downer allows you to shift pitch up and down without affecting the tempo. We recommend that these new tempo and pitch adjustment features be used with care and insight. Ideally, you will be using these recorded accompaniments and Amazing Slow Downer for practice only.

The audio quality may be somewhat compromised when played through the Amazing Slow Downer. This compromise in quality will not be a factor in playing the CD audio track on a normal CD player or through another audio computer program.

INSTALLATION INSTRUCTIONS:

For Macintosh OS 8, 9 and X:
- Load the CD-ROM into your CD-ROM Drive on your computer.
- Each computer is set up a little differently. Your computer may automatically open the audio CD portion of this enhanced CD and begin to play it.
- To access the CD-ROM features, double-click on the data portion of the CD-ROM (which will have the Hal Leonard icon in red and be named as the book).
- Double-click on the "Amazing OS 8 (9 or X)" folder.
- Double-click "Amazing Slow Downer"/"Amazing X PA" to run the software from the CD-ROM, or copy this file to your hard disk and run it from there.
- Follow the instructions on-screen to get started. The Amazing Slow Downer should display tempo, pitch and mix bars. Click to select your track and adjust pitch or tempo by sliding the appropriate bar to the left or to the right.

For Windows:
- Load the CD-ROM into your CD-ROM Drive on your computer.
- Each computer is set up a little differently. Your computer may automatically open the audio CD portion of this enhanced CD and begin to play it.
- To access the CD-ROM features, click on My Computer then right click on the Drive that you placed the CD in. Click Open. You should then see a folder named "Amazing Slow Downer". Click to open the "Amazing Slow Downer" folder.
- Double-click "setup.exe" to install the software from the CD-ROM to your hard disk. Follow the on-screen instructions to complete installation.
- Go to "Start," "Programs" and find the "Amazing Slow Downer" folder. Go to that folder and select the "Amazing Slow Downer" software.
- Follow the instructions on-screen to get started. The Amazing Slow Downer should display tempo, pitch and mix bars. Click to select your track and adjust pitch or tempo by sliding the appropriate bar to the left or to the right.
- Note: On Windows NT, 2000 and XP, the user should be logged in as the "Administrator" to guarantee access to the CD-ROM drive. Please see the help file for further information.

MINIMUM SYSTEM REQUIREMENTS:

For Macintosh:
Power Macintosh; Mac OS 8.5 or higher; 4 MB Application RAM; 8x Multi-Session CD-ROM drive

For Windows:
Pentium, Celeron or equivalent processor; Windows 95, 98, ME, NT, 2000, XP; 4 MB Application RAM; 8x Multi-Session CD-ROM drive